Be Fierce:
Poetry that Inspires, Builds,
and Ignites Champions
On and Off the Field

Be Fierce:
Poetry that Inspires, Builds and Ignites Champions On and Off the Field

BELINDER S. JACKSON, MBA, MA

Copyright © 2023 Belinder S. Jackson.
All Rights Reserved.

Be Fierce:
Poetry that Inspires, Builds, and Ignites
Champions On and Off the Field

No part of this publication may be reproduced, distributed, stored in a retrieval system, or transmitted in whole, in any form or by any means, including electronic, mechanical, photocopying, recording, or otherwise, without written permission of the author, except in the case of brief quotations with proper reference. For permission requests, write to the author, addressed, "Attention: Permissions Request" at the email address below.

ISBN: 978-1-7332705-2-6 (Hard copy)
ISBN: 978-1-7332705-0-2 (Paper copy)
ISBN: 978-1-7332705-1-9 (eBook)

Library of Congress Control Number: 2022905253

All content is a product of the author's creativity, individual experiences, and unrelenting imagination.

Content, Cover, and Interior Design: Belinder S. Jackson

For permissions requests, contact
victory@reshapingpossible.com

For more information about the author, visit:
www.reshapingpossible.com

Printed in Debary, FL U.S.A
First Edition: May 2023

I'd like to send a special thank you to my extraordinary family - my husband Allen Jackson, son Ethan Jackson, daughter Elise Jackson, mother Jeanette Stringer, my sisters Anita Martin-Jones, Vanessa Martin, Shawnda King, La'Toya Stephens, Takeemah Youngblood-Hawkins, and Katina (Shay) Master, as well as my brother Alonzo Taylor for their prayers, unconditional love, and support over the years.

Momma, thank you for all of your countless sacrifices raising your children.
The poem **"Out of the Blue"** is dedicated to you.

To my college Coach Chandra Cheeseborough, thank you for believing in me. To my softball, basketball and track coaches, godparents, godsisters, and godbrothers, thank you for supporting me.

To my friends, more like sisters,
Missy Tillman, Sabine Robinson, Juanita Jones and Tameka Hall, as well as my countless friends, and family – you know who you are,
I am my best because of you – thank you.

This book is dedicated to my children
Ethan and Elise.

Remember, with God, you can do anything;
ALL THINGS ARE POSSIBLE!

Preface:

Life is filled with ups and downs,
tides that push us out, pull us in, and sometimes
takes us under.

Be Fierce, is a compilation of thought-
provoking poems written to inspire, build, and
ignite individuals from all ages, backgrounds, and
demographics to walk boldly into their future. To be
bold, passionate, powerful, relentless, and strong.
It is meant to meet individuals where they are
and help them imagine what they
CAN BE and what they WILL DO.

Without a doubt, know that:
YOU are important.
YOU are priceless.
YOU are unique.

With every morning's rise,
let us affirm how important,
valuable, and resilient we are,
because we are!

~Belinder S. Jackson

[INSPIRED CONTENT]

Chapter 1	Accepting the Challenge	1
	Out of the BLUE	3
	I Am More	5
	My Confidence	7
	Dream	9
	That Girl	11
	That Son	15
Chapter 2	Embracing Your Opportunities	18
	What If	21
	Powerful Women	23
	Make a Commitment	25
	The Heart of a Child	27
	I Am	29
	Not Deterred	31
Chapter 3	Bringing Your Brilliance	32
	Character	35

Phenomenal Run	37
Your It!	39
Position	41
I Like Me	43
My Black Is Beautiful	45
Chapter 4 Embracing Your Best	46
Good Trouble	49
Pessimistic Soulja	51
Mended	53
We SOAR	55
My Space	57
Imagine	59
I'm Free	61
Checkmate	63
Final Thoughts and Reflections	64

Be Fierce:
Poetry that Inspires, Builds, and Ignites Champions On and Off the Field

Introduction

In a world filled with uncertainty, it is easy to become withdrawn. It is natural to get marred down in our feelings, failures, insecurities, and our fears. For some of us, we innately become anxious, and overwhelmed – causing us to feel skeptical, alone, judged, unsure, sub-par, minimized, dismissed, and/or rejected.

Though those feelings may be real at times, it does not mean that we have to lavish in those feelings, promote them, or project them – internally or externally. We do not have to remain in those dreary, dry dark places. With the right light, the right prism, the right lens, and the right perspective, we can spend more time embracing our visible and untapped brilliance.

In closing – I am challenging you to bet on yourself. Don't be afraid to fail, don't be afraid of falling, don't be afraid of hearing no, don't be afraid of making mistakes, don't be afraid to speak up, don't be afraid to stand, and above all, don't be afraid to deliver - time after time, over and over again.

Chapter 1 Accepting the Challenge

OUT OF THE BLUE

Out of the BLUE

With a glimpse of hope for the future, out of the BLUE, legacies were born, and dreams came true.

Their calculations were off,
Estimates misguided,
Hypotheses flawed,
And their predictions, wrong.
They projected what they expected, but her vision wasn't affected.

She saw more, wanted more, worked for more, and she got more.
Through every trial, every mistake, every mishap, and heartbreak,
She waded through the turbulence, and created waves, BLUE waves.

And out of the BLUE, who would have knew that a legacy of greatness was brewing, and what she fought for was not only priceless, it was well worth pursuing.

With discarded scraps she built her own stage, and today she and her family are creating waves, BLUE waves.

They doubted her, teased her, negated her, criticized her, and minimized her, but out of the BLUE, she rose, and they rose, in plain clothes OUT OF THE BLUE.

Inspired by and dedicated to my mother.

I AM MORE

I Am More

Sometimes we don't feel like who we are...
We fail to walk in our worth...
We fall short of our calling...
Appreciate our value...
And sometimes......
We willingly place our lives in neutral, waiting on a jump start
or a tow...
When God has positioned us, equipped us, and empowered
us..........
To DO more,
To SEE more, and,
To BE more.

I AM MORE.

More than my job title, my business, the position within my
organization, my financial status, and my zip code.

I AM MORE.

More than my race, my marital status, my socioeconomic
status, and my grade point average.

I AM MORE.

More than my shortcomings, my limitations, my blunders, my
mishaps, my trips, my mistakes, my falls, and my failures.

I AM MORE.

More than the things I've accomplished, the things I am
accomplishing, and the things that I shall accomplish.

I AM MORE.
Simply because God said so.
I AM MORE....

Confidence...

My Confidence

My confidence runs through my body,
My hands, my arms, and my feet,
My heart, my lungs, and of course through my speech.

It permeates my arteries, it's in my eyes,
It helps me to thrive just as the word implies.

It runs through my vocal cords as I speak,
Gives me strength when I am weak,
Because I am important, and I am unique.

It's in my shoulders, my elbows, and my gut,
I'm embracing my confidence, now watch my strut.

It's in my poise, it's in my pause, and my position,
Igniting self-confidence is my personal mission.

It's in my neck and my chin,
It's in my skin, my smile, and my grin,
That's how WE WIN.

I could go on and on,
BECAUSE MY CONFIDENCE NEVER ENDS....

Dream...

Dream

If you're going to dream,
You might as well DREAM BIG...
I mean REAL BIG...
Releasing all of the anchors, attitudes, barriers, and brakes...
Along with your anguish, your fears, and your mistakes.

Dream like you are only an arm's reach away...
Dream like there is nothing that can stand in your way.

Dream like children fighting to make their parents proud...
Dream like the relentless stars that pierce through the clouds.

Be that dream our forefathers thought of so long ago...
Be that trailblazer willing to say, I DID THAT and
I SAID SO!

That *Girl...*

That Girl

Will you be that girl who will not be denied -
That girl with blazing courage that soon will rise?

Will you be that girl who walks with incredible pride -
That girl who rises to the occasion when others step aside?

Will you be that girl who runs as hard as she can -
That girl with newfound confidence, that girl with the plan?

Tell me, will you be that girl?

Will you be that girl with passion, the one who refuses to
stand still -
That girl who just won't quit, despite how she feels?

Will you be that girl who speaks with resounding pride -
That girl who redefines possible with each and every stride?

Will you be that girl who keeps pressing though they criticize
her looks -
That same girl who is determined to author a best-selling
book?

Tell me, will you be that girl?

Will you be that girl who holds up a shield of faith -
That girl who is predestined to win her gut-wrenching race?

Will you be that girl with a profound bold voice -
That girl that tells opportunity you don't have a choice?

Tell me, will you be that girl?

Continued…

Will you be that girl who designs her own waves -
That girl who stands bravely and demands the stage?

Will you be that girl who steps up to bat -
Though socioeconomics and inequalities work to hold her
back?

Will you be that girl who is constantly becoming -
That girl who is intellectually honest, smart, and yes stunning?

Tell me, will you be that girl?

THAT GIRL

That Son...

That Son

Will you be that son who emits bravery from within -
That son who is not tossed back and forth by the wind?

Will you be that son who is encouraged, empowered and equipped -
That son who is predestined to change the world with his gifts?

Tell me, will you be that son?

Will you be that son chosen from the wound to lead -
That son who is fired up and finds ways to succeed?

Will you be that son who is confident and astute -
That son who is not distracted by what he sees others do?

Will you be that son who refuses to doubt -
That son who reminds the world not to count him out?

Will you be that son who is strategic and bold -
That son who creates the narrative, rather than simply watch it unfold?

Will you be that son who is disciplined like a clock -
That son who won't let anyone confine him to a box?

Will you be that son who knows he's number one -
That son who steps up to the plate and yes, hits a home run?

Will you be that son who lives life with passion -
That son who sees endless possibilities and focuses on what matters?

Tell me, will you be that son?

Continued…

Will you be that son who walks with his shoulders back -
That son who still smiles despite unprovoked attacks?

Will you be that son who fills the prescription for tomorrow -
That son who refuses to accept empty promises and mere
pennies on a dollar?

Will you be that son who knows his self-worth -
That son who moves with momentum and intentionally
chooses his network?

Will you be that son who is armed with a shield of faith -
That son with resilience, determined to win his race?

Tell me, will you be that son?

THAT SON

Chapter 2   Embracing Your Opportunities

What If...

What If

What if you intentionally forged your way to the
other side of if?
Through the dust-stricken valley connected to the steepest
cliff?
What if?

What if you were curious enough to risk failing, but brave
enough to stand back up?
What if you were courageous enough to bet on yourself, even
when things were blisteringly tough?
Truth is, we're more than enough.
But what if?

What if you vigorously challenged your fears, and decided to
take them under?
What if you trapped your fears in a bottle and made them feel
your thunder?
No, I didn't blunder, I just wonder.
What if?

What if you found that you were daringly different from the
rest?
What if your different, is what you needed to pass your test?
Nevertheless, I humbly digress.
But what if?

What if you pressed forward immensely with everything you
had?
What if you faced your fears with gladness, instead of being
mad?
It was just a thought that I had, about what if?

What if futures could be altered by the attitudes we emit?
What if you chose to accelerate, rather than finding ways to
quit?

Should I stand or should I sit? You're up to bat, will you hit?
Peculiar questions I must admit,
But these were questions I had about what if?

What if?

Powerful...

Powerful Women

Powerful women are the POWERHOUSE of our communities.

Their inspiration, resilience, and strength power-up listening ears and rattle resisting hearts.

Powerful women empower, expect, inspect, reflect, and digest what is important, what is meaningful, and what is necessary.

The light from their feet is lit by what was not possible and kept ablaze by what is possible.

The strength of their hands are persuaded by I can, rather than the barriers and oppression set in motion by man.

Powerful women are not perfect, but rather they act with purpose, passion, precision, and they monitor their performance.

Their value is not dictated by what people think of them, what folks say she can have, or where she is right now.

Powerful women learn the rules, then break the rules, then write new rules, because their ingenuity is their natural fuel.

Powerful women drive change; powerful women rise.
Powerful women break barriers; they will never be denied!

Commit...

Make a Commitment

Make a commitment to be excellent,
Make a commitment to be kind,
Make a commitment to change the world,
One interaction at a time.

Make a commitment to be your best,
Make a commitment to reflect,
Make a commitment to do something differently,
To help someone else.

Make a commitment to be great,
Make a commitment to show your wit,
Make a commitment to push forward,
Even when you want to quit.

Make a commitment to live,
Make a commitment to be free,
Make a commitment to remain focused,
On the things you want to see.

Make a commitment to love,
Make a commitment to pray,
Make a commitment to set boundaries,
For what you will and will not say.

Make a commitment to move forward,
Make a commitment to win,
Make a commitment to yourself,
To never settle or give in.

Heart...

The Heart of a Child

Instill in me what I shall be so I won't go astray,
Instill in me what I shall be so I won't lose my way.

Meet me where I am now, not where I am supposed to be,
Meet me where I am now, being perfect is just foreign to me.

Encourage me to be great and learn my history too,
Remind me of my future and all I will be able to do.

Encourage me to be confident, bold, and free,
My environment will not dictate what I am destined to be.

Teach me in a way that brings out the best in me,
As if I were your only child and you carried me.

Help me recover when I have made a mistake,
Remind me that 1 am brilliant, and I have what it takes.

Be that smile when I have had a difficult day,
And teach me what I should do differently to have a better
day.

Please don't give up on me, you never know who I'll be,
Your patience, love, and guidance might be just the things that
I need.

I Am...

I Am

I am bold, brave, powerful, and unique,
The laughter of nay sayers no longer define me.

I am resilient, intelligent, wise, and strong,
I will never settle for get-by-ism or a substandard platform.

I am confident, smart, poised, and free,
Challenging the status quo and destined to succeed.

I am bold, brave, powerful, and unique
Oppressors and nay sayers no longer define me.

Not Deterred...

Not Deterred

In a small factory "I Can't" got stuck in a can and put himself
on a shelf.
Frustrated by the lack of opportunity, he got tied up in a rut.

In the same factory, in a similar container, "I Can's" mind
always ran,
How can I get myself out of this vision suppressing can?

Not by deterred by similar setbacks or defeats,
"I Can" said I will not be limited by anyone - that includes me.

"I Can" kept pressing while "I Can't" looked on with doubt,
"I Can't" was shocked and amazed when "I Can" said,
"Hey Yall I'm Out!"

Chapter 3   Bringing Your Brilliance

Character...

<u>Character</u>

Character is built by calluses from putting in the work,
It is a compilation of values that showcase your worth.

Build character and humility rather than arrogance and pride,
For these are unifying qualities that will last over time.

Build courage and resilience rather than get-by-ism and defeat,
For they will take you to the next level when others shrink
back to their seats.

When I was born, I had expectations placed on me, and what a
gift they were;
They taught me how to stretch beyond what I thought was
possible and solidify my SELF-WORTH.

Run...

Phenomenal Run

For as long as I can remember, there have always been a
reason to run…
People and things to run to …
and a barrage of things to run from.

With confidence I ran around the track and sprinted down the
runway.
I commanded my fears to stand down as I boldly took my
place.

I commanded it then and I am commanding it now…
Fear you have no place in my life and definitely NOT in my
house.

I will run with excellence and expectation, persuasion, and
pride…
Reinforcing my purpose, as I press, and as I thrive.

I may slip, I may fall, and I may even drop the baton…
But nothing will stop me from completing my phenomenal
run.

Your It...

<u>Your It!</u>

Whether dressed up in a ball gown, or decked down in tennis shoes,
It's not about what I wear, my hair, or what's fair,
It's the confidence that I own and the brilliance that I share.

Who am I? Your it!

Your ace in the hole, your wild card, your draw four, your spade, your queen, your king, your full house, your four of a kind, your straight flush, and your royal flush.

Who am I?

Your hole in one, your goalkeeper, your swoosh, your home run, your first leg, your last leg, your all-star, your keynote, your first shot, and your last shot.

I am your captain, your point guard, your forward, your center, your wide receiver, your fullback, your running back, your tight end, and your quarterback.

Who am I?

I am your winning point and the confidence your fears dread to see coming......
I am your brilliant, phenomenal woman...

Better known as ...
Your It!

Position...

Position

Taking your rightful position in life, requires that we shake off a couple of things, a few situations, and a boatload of people if they aren't ready for the ride.

ME...

I Like Me

I am me, not you....... but me,
And I like me.
The extraordinary me,
The authentic me,
The one and only me.

The unrelenting me,
The groundbreaking me,
The trailblazing me,
The uniqueness of me,
And the possibilities for me.

Because I am me, not you....... but me,
And I like me.

The fearlessness of me,
The bravery of me,
The resiliency of me,
The boldness of me and guess what?
The melanin in me.

The original me,
The new me,
And the just me.

Because I am me, not you....... but me,
And I LIKE ME!

Beautiful...

My Black Is Beautiful

One thing that I've learned is that my black is beautiful.
What the world deemed impossible, we…
We made them doable…….

Denied opportunities and kept from the voting booth,
We were America's X Factor, demanding the truth.

Our freedoms on hold,
United we rose,
Our stories untold,
Our children, our brilliance,
TODAY WE BEHOLD…

Black history, black people, black dress, black suit,
I think it's about time that we give black its due.

Sophisticated, powerful, eloquent, and strong, black is the
color we all put on,
I'm rolling, I'm flowing, TOGETHER we'll win,
Oh how I'm loving my beautiful skin!

Chapter 4   Embracing Your Best

GOOD
Trouble...

Good Trouble

Listen, when you call my name,
Call it clearly, with conviction, adoration, and respect.

If you must call me trouble,
Call me GOOD TROUBLE,
Good and necessary trouble,
Call me a game changer, daughter, wife, sister, aunt, and a
mother.

I fully understand where you want to be,
but you can't get there without people like me.

Sit back and think about the POWER of SHE.
Imagine what could be done with the POWER of WE!

So, if you must call me trouble,
Call me GOOD TROUBLE,
Good and necessary trouble,
Call me a game changer, daughter, wife, sister, aunt, and a
mother.

Souljas Rise...

Pessimistic Soulja

Hey Pessimistic Soulja with your arms crossed tight,
If you loosen them up a little, you might be alright.

How you gonna be ready for battle when you train yourself to lose?
Battles ain't won by Soulja's who take pride in hitting snooze.

If you go into battle and loose, that's fine,
But give yourself a fighting chance by investing in your mind.

It is your choice, your voice, your opportunity, your time,
It's your gift to harness, your journey not mine.

I challenge you to sit up and roll your shoulders back,
And show the world what it looks like to get back on track.

Sizzle sizzle, snap pop,
I see you rising to the TOP!

MENDED...

Mended

Born into a broken city, a broken neighborhood, a broken
home, and a broken family,
All I could see were broken pieces…

When I woke up, I heard brokenness
When I daydreamed, I imagined brokenness…
When I tried to focus, I felt brokenness, and
When I slept, I saw brokenness…
Until I gave myself permission to break the cycle…

I decided that my success was not limited to the most
successful person on my block, my city, or my state.
It was my life and my future that was at stake…
Asleep, but awake, I wasn't a mistake.
I just needed a pause, a mental health break.

I began reading more, listening more, and focusing on what
matters,
I took a leap outside of my comfort zone despite all the
chatter…

I began taking feedback, realizing that I wasn't perfect,
This enabled me to find joy in perfecting my purpose.
I saw myself for who I am, a chosen servant with purpose…

A human capable of failing and making mistakes…
A human willing to champion my rightful place.

SOAR...

We SOAR

Barriers distract us,
Hurdles perplex us,
Pits constrain us,
But they don't define us.

It's our moment, our mission,
Our time, our vision.
Our trajectory, our voice,
Our mission, our choice.

Like eagles, we SOAR,
Rekeying locks and dismantling doors.
With no regrets, we SOAR!

MY Space...

My Space

Ain't no better place than where I'm standing.
This is my space, I'm commanding.
My respect, I'm demanding.
My influence, it's expanding.
My existence, outstanding.

More than the sum of my parts, I'm protecting my peace.
The world has a lot to offer, but it ain't got nothing on me.

God is my appraiser,
He assigned my worth at birth.
What you think about me, has no influence on my self-worth.

The work, I put it in.
So, I can smile, so I can grin.
Don't look for me to hold back.
I can't pretend.
They can't comprehend.
Self-hate, a dead end.

Some appreciate the skin I'm in,
The space I'm in,
I'm a good friend,
I'm not a taker, I'd rather lend.

Ain't no better place than where I'm standing,
This is my space, I'm commanding.
My respect, I'm demanding.
My influence, it's expanding.
My existence, outstanding.

Working on my Grammy.
Hall of Fame, you name it.
My name, gone frame it.
My confidence can't tame it.

This is MY SPACE!

IMAGINE...

<u>Imagine</u>

Imagine if we held the line on fear.
We took away its influence, its strength, its grip, and its sting.
Imagine if we took away its authority by invoking our courage
and our power.

Just imagine....

Imagine if fear no longer controlled our thoughts, our minds,
and our tongues,
Our choices, our behaviors, and our heartbeat...
Now that's deep...
We are STRONG, not weak...
So, let's strategically choose our words and monitor our
speech......

Imagine what we could DO.
Imagine where we could GO.
Imagine what we could BE.
Now close your eyes and IMAGINE WITH ME.

JUST IMAGINE!

FREE!

I'm Free

Some people say there is no me without you…
I say, I am not free without me.
I can't be you and still be me.
WHEN I'M ME, I'M FREE.

I'm not afraid of what I see,
Nor am I afraid of what I can't see.
I'm celebrating the best parts of me.
Everything that's perfect and everything that's not.
Shortcomings are nuggets, not simply roadblocks.

It's about what I am,
Never about what I'm not.
My momentum doesn't stop.
Fresh lines, I gotta drop.
My confidence, I rock.
Time is short, tic tock.
If you must hate, grab your mop.
Cause this sister got it locked.

Life pushed me to the edge,
I didn't drop.
I recalibrated in the valley,
Now reciting from the hilltop.
Putting on workshops.
My brilliance, non-stop.
Listen from your seat or from your rooftop.
This sister popped the top.
Juneteenth's promise unlocked.
Did you hear the mic drop?

Some people say there is no me without you…
I say, I am not free without me.
I can't be you and still be me.
WHEN I'M ME, I'M FREE.

Checkmate!

Checkmate

Some people are as real as they can be but are still fake.
But it's the man in the mirror that they love to hate.
A shadow that they try to elude, but they can't shake.
But their place, I won't take.
Their energy, I terminate.
In my own lane, I perpetually elevate.
Courageously whispering – checkmate.

FINAL THOUGHTS AND REFLECTIONS

Wherever you are, know that God has a plan and a purpose for your life; he will supply you with everything you need to accomplish your mission.

Your trials make room for your testimonies.

Make time for your talents, skills, gifts, and abilities and they will make room for you.

Reflect on your past, be mindful of where you are, and don't be afraid to take ownership of your future.

Making mistakes, failing, and coming short of our goals is part of the learning process; embrace the journey.

Keep pushing and continue making progress.

Don't be afraid to keep bringing your brilliance!

Finally, never say what you can't do,
prove to yourself what you can do and
CELEBRATE YOUR VICTORIES ALONG THE WAY.

IN MY FEARLESS FUTURE, I SEE
Write down your directional goals and aspirations.

TO CREATE MY FEARLESS FUTURE, I NEED TO
Write down what you need to create the future you envision.

THESE PEOPLE AND THINGS WILL KEEP ME
MOTIVATED AND FOCUSED

Write down who and what will help keep
you encouraged along the way.

MY SUCCESS STORIES OVER THE YEARS
Find reasons to be thankful and give yourself credit.
Write down your achievements (large and small) over the years.
Be sure to get feedback from friends, family, mentors, teachers,
professors, coaches, trainers, etc. Thereafter, periodically review
this list and continue documenting your incredible journey.

MORE OF MY SUCCESS STORIES OVER THE YEARS

MORE OF MY SUCCESS STORIES OVER THE YEARS

MORE OF MY SUCCESS STORIES OVER THE YEARS

MORE OF MY SUCCESS STORIES OVER THE YEARS

MORE OF MY SUCCESS STORIES OVER THE YEARS

Made in the USA
Monee, IL
12 May 2023